THE ONE THING THAT
IS LIMITING YOU...
AND HOW TO CONQUER IT

DEVIN SCHADT

Excerpts from the English translation of the
Catechism of the Catholic Church, Second Edition,
©1994, 1997, 2000 by Libreria Editrice Vaticana,
United States Catholic Conference, Washington, D.C.
All rights reserved.

Unless otherwise noted,
Scripture quotations are from
the Douay-Rheims version of Sacred Scripture.
Copyright 1914 by John Murphy Company

Cover Design: Devin Schadt

© 2020 by Devin Schadt
All right reserved.

ISBN: 978-1-7327739-9-8
Printed in the United States.

Stewardship: A Mission of Faith
11 BlackHawk Lane
Elizabethtown, PA 17022
StewardshipMission.org

Contents

It's Robbing You ... of You? **7**

1.

Where Do Your Fears Come From? **21**

2.

Good and Bad Fears **41**

3.

The Six Consequences of Fear **57**

4.

Conquering F.E.A.R. with R.I.S.K. **117**

It's Robbing You . . . of You

The man who never mustered the courage to ask his longtime girlfriend to marry him remains a bachelor to this day. The woman whose hyper concern with complications caused by childbirth and the potential of pain regrets that she never bore children of her own. The young man who always wanted to do martial arts, but because he believes himself to be weak, instead plays

InterFEARence

video games to this day. The man in his mid-forties who boasts of training for the ever-upcoming marathon, but never does because he thinks he will fail. The miserable employee who is "doing his time" until he retires because he never followed his dream of launching his own start-up venture. The woman who has written several manuscripts but refuses to submit them to a publisher because she might be rejected. The wife who discovers that her husband is unfaithful, but neglects to confront him because she is sure that he will leave her. The man who rarely gives to the less fortunate because he may need the money later. The homeowner who doesn't have the guts to tell her neighbor to pick up after his dog poops in her yard because she avoids conflict. The yes-man employee who shies from telling his boss what he really thinks because he worried about being demoted. The person who rarely accepts invitations to

It's Robbing You ... of You

social events because he feels awkward and may not "fit in." The woman who complains about being stuck in a relationship with a verbally abusive boyfriend but lacks the courage to break it off and go it alone.

What does each person in this litany of personal regret have in common? Each allowed a hidden, underlying factor to dictate their decisions and ultimately dominate the trajectory of his or her life. What is this nearly imperceptible factor that has the tremendous power to run and ruin our lives?

FEAR.

F.E.A.R. can be defined as **F**eelings/**E**motions **A**ttacking **R**eason. Fear becomes debilitating and undermines, mitigates, and in some cases, destroys, our ability to live in hope. Submission to fear allows our feelings and emotions to attack, suppress, and overrule our ability to reason properly. When we permit emotions and feelings to override our ability to reason and make decisions with wisdom and logic, we gradually become imprisoned in fear.

For example, years ago I took my eldest daughter to Estes Park, Colorado, to celebrate her graduation from high school. The plan was to do some hiking and sightseeing, including the scenic drive through Rocky Mountains National Park on Trail Ridge Road. Trail Ridge Road is one of the most popular scenic drives in Colorado, the highest continuously paved road in the United Sates.

When I was around eight, my dad took our family to the Rockies in our Ford Club Wagon family van. Somewhere in Colorado we ascended a thin, one-lane, barely paved road, with hairpin curves and no guardrails. On the driver's side, the steep mountainside was so close I thought I could extend my hand and touch it. On the

It's Robbing You ... of You

other side was an incredible precipice that appeared to have no bottom. At one point, my dad realized that we couldn't take the van any higher. His only choice was to drive in reverse down the mountain until we could find a broader place to do a three-point turn. My mother became anxious and my father became extraordinarily quiet. Overcome by fear, I laid on the floor, refusing to look out the window. That experience, combined with my fear of heights, was imbedded deep into my psyche.

The drive with my daughter up Trail Ridge Road was exhilarating and, honestly, unsettling. The expansive views from the lookouts were breathtaking. However, the sharp turns, my fear of heights, the lack of guardrails, and the foreboding forecast of freezing rain and snow caused me to internally freak out.

Imagine my eighteen-year-old daughter, who up to this point believed me to be her courageous hero who was unafraid of nearly anything, sitting in the passenger seat with her old man, who, clenching the steering wheel, was becoming increasingly debilitated by his dread of falling off of the mountainside.

We pulled the car over at the last lookout before the drive up and over the peak of Trail Ridge Road. We stepped out of the car, took in the majestic view, took a couple of cameos, and then I turned to her and confessed, "Honey, I don't think we're going up any farther today." After settling back in the car I explained to her that the sleet, snow, and my lame fear of heights had gotten the best of me.

As we descended the mountain, a sickening feeling of dismay pervaded my soul. I knew that I had failed. And worse, so did my daughter. To enhance the experience of my personal limitedness, within one year, while on her honeymoon, my daughter's young, courageous,

It's Robbing You ... of You

newlywed husband drove her over the Rockies on that same road. Ugh.

I had gone only so far. I'd ascended only so high before turning back, retreating in defeat. I was afraid to scale the heights, and because I gave my feelings permission to override reason I was conquered by fear and never saw the glorious, breathtaking views that awaited . . . and neither did my daughter, until my son-in-law completed the mission that I could not.

It is true that I could try to justify my actions by arguing that my childhood experiences and my innate fear of heights limited me. And that may be true. Reason, however, told me that there was nothing to fear. Tens of thousands of people drive safely over Trail Ridge Road annually. I myself have driven through countless snowstorms, streets sheeted in ice, and sleet storms that prevented my windshield wipers from working properly.

Nevertheless, I survived. But that day, while with my daughter, I allowed my emotions to overtake my ability to reason, and because of that *I chose* not to ascend, to succeed, to achieve my goal. Furthermore, not only did I disappoint myself, but I also disappointed my daughter.

We all have "mountains" to climb. We all have destinies that we desire to achieve. We all have, or should have, or once had, lofty goals. Yet, fear can cause massive, uninvited, *inter**fear**ence*, in our careers, relationships, child-rearing, marriages, financial endeavors, home ownership, our ability to be generous, and especially in our relationship with God and the great mission He has given to us.

Rather than pressing on in our ascent up the "mountain," we allow fear to grow in our soul. We give it a home. We grant it permission it to take root and vine. We permit it to cover the walls of our heart. We then blame the fear as the reason we failed. Why? Because

It's Robbing You ... of You

all we can see is the vine of fear and not the beauty of the soul that it is covering. In other words, we no longer believe that we are to blame for not overcoming our fears; we believe that our fears are to blame for overcoming us.

Fear is like the background noise of the television or radio. You know that the noise is there, that it exists, but you tune it out and learn to live with it. You build your life around it, never changing the channel or the volume, and fail to shut it off altogether. Eventually the lyrics of the songs and the negativity of sensationalistic news creeps in and lodges itself deep within your thoughts. You say to yourself, "Of course it doesn't affect me." But over time a kinship with these voices develops. The kinship eventually becomes dependency, and the dependency eventually becomes belief, and the belief eventually determines how you live.

Similarly, the voice of fear, which is continually playing in the background, argues for a platform inside your head. It wants to be heard. It wants to be believed. But not only believed but obeyed. When you obey fear your belief systems are compromised. You become debilitated and your ability to take prudential risk is dramatically hindered.

One of the chief reasons why fear dominates our decisions and conditions our life's trajectory is because we fail to address it. We inadvertently, or sometimes purposefully, neglect to face it. To overcome fear, it is imperative that we confront it head on, identify it, and determine a way to manage it. For if we cannot master fear, fear will master us. Fear, if given permission to reign in your brain, will suffocate your true, God-given identity and restrain you from achieving your God-given destiny. Fear is one of your greatest enemies.

It's Robbing You ... of You

When I was in high school, the Presidential Fitness Award was a big deal. It honored students who achieved an outstanding level of physical fitness. The test was comprised of six activities: curl-ups, pull-ups, push-ups, and sit-ups; the 30-foot shuttle-run, and the 1-mile endurance run.

I surpassed all the benchmarks in every category except one: the pull-up. Around the sixth grade, I attempted to do a pull-up in gym class but failed. Embarrassed, I concluded that my body was not designed to do pull-ups and I never gave it a second chance. I continued to do push-ups, sit-ups, shuttle-runs, and long-distance running because I was skilled at these exercises.

My high school gym teacher targeted me as one of his students who would win the Presidential Fitness Award, but when it came time to shine, I shied away from the invitation for fear of failure.

InterFEARence

It wasn't until I was in my early forties that a friend mentioned that a significant part of his daily training routine included pull-ups. He didn't look like he could do push-ups let alone pull-ups. I confessed that I had never been able to do them. His mouth dropped. Then he said, "Just get a pull-up bar and do it."

I overcame my fear, purchased a bar, installed it, and did my best to do a pull-up. But I couldn't. It was humiliating. But around that time, I began incorporating planks into my training routine. The planks activated certain muscle groups that were previously dormant. Soon, I was able to struggle through five pull-ups. Today, I'm almost fifty and can knock out fifteen to twenty pull ups on a good day, and all my workouts include multiple sets of pull-ups, curl-ups, and chin-ups. I faced my fears and eventually accomplished a lifelong goal.

Where Do Your Fears Come From?

Fear can keep us from taking healthy risks, trying new things, meeting new people, asking for forgiveness, being generous, challenging ourselves, getting married and having a family, accepting and learning from failure, standing up for the less fortunate, defending the truth, or surrendering our lives to God.

But this is important: Fear can only hinder us *if we choose to allow it to become a dominating, force in our lives.*

On the other hand, by overcoming F.E.A.R. we can begin to experience the courage and liberation necessary to be the person God has designed and destined us to be. This is precisely what is at stake: your ability to be who God has made you to be, which means your ability to be happy, and your ability to affect others. In other words, fear—if you allow it—could keep you from taking risks for God and bringing His presence to others. If this happens, fear makes a person's life utterly miserable, a lifelong, self-imposed imprisonment.

In this little book, I hope to help you overcome F.E.A.R so that you can experience the freedom for which Christ gave His life. To accomplish this, I will explain where fear comes from; the four types of fear, and explain which are essentially good and necessary, and which will undermine your ability to thrive; the six negative consequences of fear; and lastly, a compelling strategy to conquer the enemy of fear and live a life of godly liberation.

This does not mean that you will become a daredevil and parachute out of skyscrapers or jump from one highrise roof to another. But if we apply the simple, doable principles outlined in the following pages, we will move from being imprisoned in our fears to unlocking God's power in our lives and becoming a grace-filled force, of faith, hope, and the love of Christ in the lives of others.

1.

Where Do Your Fears Come From?

A longtime friend was given a new assignment at one of his corporation's satellite branches. The purpose of their first team meeting was to introduce themselves to one another and become acquainted with my friend, their new boss. During the meeting, the office manager of seven years invited everyone to tell a little about themselves. He thought it would be

InterFEARence

a good idea for each person to state their name, the amount of time they'd been with the company, and their biggest fear.

It seemed innocent enough. One of the employees jumped in with "spiders." Everyone chuckled. Another person, giving my friend a sharp look, retorted "unemployment." More laughter. Then another person chimed in with "death." Artificial chuckles. Then another responded, "Not belonging." Awkward silence. The exercise had just gotten deep.

Fifteen years ago, while sitting around a table at a local coffee shop with a group of friends who comprised our local writers' group, one of the guys turned to me and asked, "What are you afraid of?" Three responses flooded my brain simultaneously. First, "There is no way I am giving you a real answer." Second, "How long do you have?" Third, "I have a fear of questions like

Where Do Your Fears Come From?

yours." The truth is that I am afraid of a lot. Further, those fears reveal much about who I am, and therefore I'd rather not reveal them.

Why is it that when we reveal our fears, we feel vulnerable and exposed? The reason is that nearly every fear is deeply rooted in the potential loss, or the actual loss, of something we hold dear. In other words, *you can know what a person loves by what he or she fears losing.*

By knowing someone's fears you are peeking under their hood. You gain access to their heart and what they love. Motion picture producers capitalize on this truth. The antagonist finds out what the protagonist loves, and afterward seizes it and holds it for ransom, until the protagonist surrenders and complies with the antagonist's agenda.

The person at my friend's meeting who responded to the question "What do you fear?" with "Not belonging" is revealing something profound about himself. He's disclosing that he is afraid of not having friends, of not being a part of a community, of not being important to others.

At first, it appears that he is simply afraid of what he *could* lose: potential friends and a potential community. But the reality is that he's afraid of losing his current friends and losing future friendships. On a deeper level, he's afraid of not being important, which indicates that he is afraid of losing his self-importance.

The person who is afraid of failure is actually fearful of losing his personal honor. The person who fears success is actually fearful of the change that comes with success, and the potential loss of the success he's achieved. Almost twenty-five years ago the lottery had peaked at some ginormous dollar amount. I and four other employees combined our money to purchase

Where Do Your Fears Come From?

a host of tickets. After we returned to the office, my coworker considered that if we won, we would have to surrender half of the winnings to state, and then, after splitting the kitty five ways, he would have a measly pile of cash. After he paid off his debt, purchased his vacation homes, yacht, and sports cars, he might not have enough money to retire immediately and live off of the winnings until he died—around the age of 100. Poor guy. He became fearful of losing what he didn't even have.

The fear of being judged is actually the fear of losing a good reputation or honor among peers, or the loss of the security of being "right." The fear of self-improvement or self-challenge is actually a fear of losing control, or a fear of failure, which is fearing the loss of one's honor. The fear of losing control is just that: the loss of being in control.

When a person fears not having enough time to complete his project, he is actually fearful of losing, or "wasting," time. Even the fear of the "unknown" is a fear of losing the "known." As one psychologist puts it, "You cannot fear something that you do not know. Nobody is afraid of the unknown. What you really fear is the loss of the known."

The fear of illness is actually the fear of losing one's health. The fear of financial ruin is the fear of losing one's security. The fear of death is the fear of losing one's life. The fear of hell is actually the fear of losing heaven. You get the idea. *Fear is nearly always connected to the loss of something that we deem valuable or important.*

Let's return to the question: What are you afraid of? Or more precisely, what are you afraid of losing? It is difficult to answer that question when things are operating as planned rather than when things are malfunc-

Where Do Your Fears Come From?

tioning. Perhaps a mental exercise can help us amplify the idea of fear being connected with loss.

Political people often focus on "rights." The rights of the nation, the rights of the citizens, our declared constitutional rights. Rights and their associated political parties are emotional hotbeds.

For example, a person believes in the right to bear arms, while another believes in suppressing that right. Both, on the surface, have a similar goal: to protect people's lives. Both have polar opposite ways to achieve that goal. A woman believes that abortion is simply her "choice," which allows her to live life to the full, while another woman believes that a woman does not have the choice to destroy an unborn baby's life. Both want what every human, including the child in the womb, will want: the freedom to live and have life. A homosexual couple believes that marriage can be between two people of the same sex, and yet will oppose those who believe that marriage is between people of the opposite sex. A parent believes that child porn is a perversion of human sexuality and the worst kind of child abuse, while another believes that he has a right to produce or watch child porn as an expression of his or her personal sexual identity, though such an act is not only criminal but immoral. A person believes in freedom of religion, while another uses their freedom to ensure that religious freedom does not exist.

We could fill books with examples of rights-based feuds. Regardless of what side you are on, every person who takes a side has one thing in common: they are afraid of losing that which they believe is, or should be, rightfully theirs. The potential loss of these rights can cause their feelings and emotions to become volatile and violent.

Where Do Your Fears Come From?

Fear of loss, which is often based upon imaginary outcomes, if left unchecked can escalate into demonizing another human being for their opposing beliefs. Considering this, ask yourself: Who do I blame for my problems? Who is my enemy? Who do I demonize as my nemesis? By identifying those persons, authorities, and institutions that we blame for robbing us of our rights, we begin to identify what we are actually afraid of losing, which helps us to identify more clearly what we fear the most. This is important because such fears cripple our progress and limits our ability to be who God has designed us to be.

Fear proceeds from a loss of something and that fear of loss is proportionate to our attachment to what we are afraid of losing. In other words, the level of emotion connected to the possible loss of something indicates how much you love that something. Whenever we are threatened with the removal of what we love our fear increases.

Between the moment we are threatened with losing something and the actual removal of that loved object, our imagination begins to invent all sorts of wicked outcomes. The longer the time between the threat of loss and the time of the actual loss, the more time our imagination has to conceive the worst results.

It is during this "imaginative" period that doubt will often invade our being, usually at a deep spiritual level. Doubt instills a mistrust of others and ultimately of God, His plan, and His goodness.

For example, in the account of the fall of Adam and Eve, the evil one suggested to Eve that "God doth know that in what day soever you shall eat therefore, your eyes shall be opened: and you shall be as Gods knowing good and evil" (Gen 3:5).

Where Do Your Fears Come From?

The evil one instills doubt in Eve's heart. What is this doubt? That their eyes are closed, and that God has kept them in darkness. If only they could bypass God and His command, then their eyes would be open, and they could see and be as God.

Notice that the devil instills a doubt from which a fear proceeds. Doubt and fear go hand in hand. It is not conclusive which comes first; but it is certain that there will never be one without another. When St. Peter accepted Christ's invitation for him to walk on the water, he suddenly "saw the wind" and began to sink. After the Lord saved Peter, He poignantly asked him, "O you of little faith, why did you doubt?" (Mt 14:31). Peter became afraid of drowning and began to doubt. Fear instilled doubt, and doubt escalated the fear. Both fear and doubt are inseparable, like evil, conjoined twin sisters. If you have one, you certainly have the other.

Both fear and doubt are born from the potential of losing something we love. In Eve's case, the loss of being like God. The potential of losing something we love instills doubt, which incites our imagination, which consequently agitates feelings and emotions, which subsequently attack and undermine our ability to reason properly. When feelings and emotions handcuff our ability to think with the mind of Christ, who is Logos, logic Himself, we begin to mistrust others and ultimately God and His goodness.

When this mistrust of God, of His goodness, and of His will take hold, we will do whatever is demanded of us to keep from losing what we love. We begin to believe that God is against our happiness and therefore we must take matters into our own hands. When this occurs, it is a certain sign that we have erected an idol in our hearts. We have set up a creaturely image in the place of our Creator. We have decided to love and adore the creature above the Creator who is Love.

When we do this, we are loving the wrong things and loving things wrongly. This type of fear, according to St. Thomas Aquinas, is a sin. St. Thomas explains that every sin involves an inordinate love, an inordinate desire, an inordinate vice, and an *inordinate fear*. In other words, if we love something in the wrong way, we make it more important than God and God's will for our lives. This is unreasonable, and it is sin. But don't miss this point: every sin involves fear, and fear can be a sin. (We will discuss good and bad fears in the next chapter).

Reason tells us that there is a hierarchical order of loves: first God; second our soul and the soul of our neighbor; third our body; and lastly, our possessions.[1]

We love first what loves us first. Since God loves us first, we are to love God first, and above all things, even above our family members, our freedom, our personal rights, our country, and our friends. Yet, when we love God first, God allows us to love our family, friends, and ourselves more than we could on our own.

Reason also tells us that we are to love our soul second to loving God. Therefore, anything that is at the service of harmonizing our souls with God and His holy will is most important and most logical. Why? Because it is illogical and unreasonable to love something that will lead you away from the One who alone can give you supreme happiness. We love ourselves truly by loving God who truly loves us; and we love God, ourselves, and our neighbor by doing what is best for our souls.

Reason also tells us that after loving God first, and our soul and our neighbor's soul second, we are to love our body third. A proper love of the body includes physical and mental health. This love for the body can

Where Do Your Fears Come From?

easily become disordered. Lastly, we are to care for our possessions. When the fear of losing our possessions, or our health, or the grandeur of our body compromises our willingness to follow God and His will, we have committed idolatry. We are loving our body or our possessions more than the God who gave us our body and our possessions.

What we love the most becomes increasingly evident when we face grave evil. When evil poses the threat of persecution, the confiscation of property, the removal of freedoms and rights, the temptation to bow down to and compromise with the devil becomes very real.

This is the strategy of the evil one. He studies you. He identifies those things that you have come to love the most. After he knows that you are deeply bonded to these creatures (meaning anything created: human beings, objects, possessions etc.), he poses the temptation: the either-or scenario. He gives you the option of following God, which could cost you your possessions, your health, your status, and even your family, or the option of keeping those things, if you only deny God. Again, it is not logical to raise something above God, because it was God who gave it to you in the first place.

I write this as the Covid-19 virus and the insanity that surrounds it continues to plague the world. It appears that the pandemic is not so much the problem as much as our reaction to it. The most volatile and vociferous reactions are connected to the issue of wearing masks. Some people are afraid that by wearing a mask they are caving to a new totalitarian, socialistic agenda, whose aim is to rob American citizens of their political and religious freedoms. Among this group exist a minority of individuals who ridicule and mock those who wear masks or are in support of wearing masks.

Where Do Your Fears Come From?

These individuals will neglect to attend Sunday Mass if they have to wear a mask. Recently, an acquaintance of mine posted on Facebook his thoughts regarding mask wearing: if you need to wear a mask, wear it but don't shame others for not wearing one. If you don't wear a mask, don't shame those who wear one for wearing one. To which another acquaintance, whom I formerly respected, retorted, "Thank you Little Nazi."

On the other hand, there are those individuals who are so fearful of contracting the Covid virus that they wear a mask while at home alone, or while driving alone in a car. I recently saw a man driving his convertible with a mask on. At the speed he was driving, I doubt that he could catch his own germs. I have witnessed people in this group yell at those who don't wear masks, condemning them of being insensitive, selfish, and uncaring.

But if both of these types of people become so entrenched in their fear of losing what they love, whether it is American freedom or their health, that they allow their feelings and emotions to attack and undermine their ability to love God above their own lives and their own freedom, and to love and respect their neighbors as they love themselves, they have fallen prey to the sin of idolatry and may be losing the only One who can supply them with supreme bliss. In this, fear becomes sinful. Like Peter, they only see the waves and the potential loss of their own lives, rather than fixing their eyes on Christ and keeping them there.

Freedom and health are great God-given goods. Yet, sometimes we can inadvertently love the creature above the Creator, and the very thing that God gave us for the purpose of leading us to Him could become the very thing that leads us away from Him. When we cannot

Where Do Your Fears Come From?

detach ourselves from what is supposed to attach us to God, then that thing becomes an idol; and rather than attaching us to God, we become bound by the fear of losing it. In other words, we fear losing the gift more than we fear losing the Giver of the gift.

So where does fear come from? The devil instills a doubt in the human heart that is intended to fuel a mistrust of God. This doubt excites the imagination to believe that the loss of something we love is imminent. This fear of losing what we love can excite our feelings and emotions and overcome our ability to think with the mind of Christ. But if we "put on the mind of Christ" (see 1 Cor 2:16; Rom 12:2; Phil 2:5) we will believe His words: "Fear is useless. What is needed is faith" (Mk 5:36).

2.

Good and Bad Fears

Fearless. The very word evokes strength, courage, honor, and resilience. Conditioned by film producers, we tend to think that being brave means having no fear. The truth is that courageous people have fears too. The difference between the fearful and the valiant is that the person bound by fear fails to manage, and overcome his fears, whereas the brave man does.

As one psychologist put it, "It's not a stretch to say that people who truly have no fear are either sociopaths or have severe brain damage. For the rest of us, being 'fearless' means knowing how to leverage fear."[2]

If fear is a common reality that even the most courageous people contend with, it will benefit us greatly to understand which types of fear we can leverage for our benefit, and which types of fears can intimidate and prevent us from fulfilling a task, a mission, or our calling. It is essential that we know the difference between good and evil fears.

Unfortunately, most of us place fear into one category rather than differentiating between those that are harmful and those that are beneficial. When we fail to make this distinction, we can erroneously label ourselves as fearful, or worse, fail to identify our fears, or why we are afraid, and fail to make the proper adjustments to overcome those fears that are evil and deter us from being all-in for God.

In other words, we need to understand clearly the difference between fears that can lead us toward God and the fulfillment of our divine calling, and fears that can hinder us from living in the peace and freedom of communion with God.

According to St. Thomas Aquinas, there are four fundamental types of fear: instinctual (natural), servile, filial, and worldly.[3] Instinctual fear is characterized by an instant reaction to something that alarms us. Instinctual fear is at the service of survival. It is hardwired into our DNA. God has designed us to be genetically predisposed to fear certain things like snakes, the edge of cliffs, wild cubs who are near their mother, house fires, and loaded guns aimed at our heads.

InterFEARence

Instinctual fear is like a home alarm system that warns you that a threat is at hand. As one psychologist puts it, "Fear is hardwired into your brain and for a good reason: Neuroscientists have identified distinct networks that run from the depths of the limbic system all the way to the prefrontal cortex and back. When these networks are electrically or chemically stimulated, they produce fear, even in the absence of a fearful stimulus. Feeling fear is neither abnormal nor a sign of weakness. The capacity to be afraid is a part of normal brain function. In fact, a lack of fear may be a sign of serious brain damage."[4]

When you are alerted to jump between an oncoming car and your daughter, who is in its path, that's instinctual fear. You instinctually fear her death. Years ago, while taking a Sunday afternoon nap, I was startled by my wife screaming, "Al is being killed! Devin help!" My

Good and Bad Fears

wife, peering out of an upstairs back window, caught sight of a struggle occurring in our neighbor's backyard. A large young man was choking our neighbor Al, while bashing the back of his head against the brick pavers that edged his garden bed. In that moment, instinctual fear acted like an alarm clock (as did my wife's high-pitched screaming) and rocketed me out of bed. Without even considering what I was actually doing, I bolted past my wife down the stairwell and out the front door, cut across our front lawn, and scaled Al's picket privacy fence. Suddenly, I found myself inside his backyard yelling at the maniac to get the #!*%* off Al. To my surprise, he did so promptly. Then he began moving toward me. Reality set in. I realized that I was stuck in a cage match with a man nearly twice my size. As I looked at Al, who appeared to be dead, instinctual fear kicked in again. I yelled at the assailant, demanding that he get out. God must have allowed this dude to see my guardian angel. His eyes widened, he suddenly did an about-face, sprinted across Al's backyard, hurdled the west fence, and disappeared. Instinctual fear caused me, without even realizing it, to risk my life for the purpose of saving Al.

Instinctual fear can also be learned by our experiences with pain or suffering. From our earliest days we are taught, or learn the hard way, not to touch the iron or the stove top while they are hot. We learn not to wander into the deep end of a pool or a river for fear of drowning. I have been burned and have nearly drowned, and both experiences were frightening enough to teach me to avoid those dangers in the future.

But instinctual fear can restrain us from entering a house that is on fire for the purpose of saving the neighbor's child, or from jumping into a river to save someone who is drowning. It is for this reason that instinctual fear is morally neutral.[5] It is neither good nor bad, but is necessary for survival. Instinctual fear becomes good when it leads us to a moral good, and it is bad when it leads us to commit a moral evil, even a sin of omission.

The second type of fear is servile fear, the fear of being punished. An example of servile fear is the person who attends Mass on Sunday simply because he fears that if he misses his "Sunday obligation" God will condemn him to hell. The distinction between servile fear and a holy fear of God is that the person who is influenced by servile fear obeys parents, authorities, and God because of his fear of being punished and the pain associated with that punishment, *not* because of his love of God.

Servile fear is not a gift of the Holy Spirit, but is substantially good and can lead us to the good. It is foundational to our relationship with parents, employers, authorities, and God. For example, I'm running late for work and am gravely tempted to run a red light. However, I notice that ahead there is a police car pulled over on the side of the road. I refrain from running the red light and obey the law, not because I love the law, or the police, or my fellow drivers, but because I fear being ticketed and fined. Yes, the outcome is good (nobody was injured), but my motivation was fear; it was not the ultimate good.

Servile fear is substantially good if it eventually leads to filial fear, a holy fear of God. But if it does not evolve into a relational holy fear, that is, the fear of disappointing or hurting the friendship between two persons, it becomes servility. which is evil.[6]

A person bound by servility obeys slavishly to avoid hell but doesn't necessarily long for heaven. Such a person does not love God, but only loves themselves and the absence of torment.

Good and Bad Fears

To help us visualize servile fear, imagine a bell curve. The bell curve begins at the lower left-hand side of the graph and ascends upward, in this case toward God. However, if servile fear is not transformed into filial fear, it eventually levels and then descends toward the bottom right corner of the graph. When this happens, servile fear plummets into slavish, scrupulous, legalistic fear of God. At this point, the relationship between God and man is master-slave instead of Father-son.

People who never ascend to filial fear and remain bound by servile fear have the tendency to become legalistic pharisees. They appear very religious and knowledgeable about their particular religion. Their chief focus is not on allowing religion to foster a relationship with God their Father, but rather understanding religion as rules and regulations. When people use laws, rules, and disciplines as the benchmarks for holiness, they fall into the trap of "rating" their own and others' level of holiness. This inevitably leads to judgmentalism, harsh criticism, and condemnation of others.

Many a person bound by servile fear has undermined Christ's Gospel, deforming and reducing it to a code of religious regulations. Servile fear causes us to focus on the obstacle of evil rather than on the goodness of God. Rather than thanking and praising God for His lavish generosity, the person bound by servile fear becomes scrupulous, believing that the simple pleasures of life (which God has given) are fatalistic traps laced with sin. Ask yourself: do I focus more on evil and sin, or on God and His goodness? In heaven the saints do not dwell on sin. Their sole focus is praising the goodness and glory of God. Saints graduate from servile fear and live in filial fear.

St. Thomas tells us that servile fear lacks the character of charity and therefore if one remains in this state of fear, he will eventually lack love itself.[7]

The third type of fear, filial fear, is from God and is identified by Scripture and confirmed by the Church as one of the seven gifts of the Holy Spirit.[8] The purpose of filial fear is to draw us ever more deeply into communion with God our Father.

Unlike servile fear, whose object of focus is punishment, filial fear's object is not to disappoint or hurt a loved one. Filial fear inspires a person with a holy fear of displeasing the one whom she loves. She is not concerned with being punished by the one who loves her, but rather, she is concerned about damaging or losing her friendship with the one she loves.

A wife who trusts that her husband loves her may refrain from telling him that he is getting fat; not because she is afraid that he will punish her, but because she is afraid that her words could hurt or displease the one she loves.

Filial fear is holy, from God, and the type of fear that helps us foster trust in relationships, especially with God. Withstanding evil by overcoming sin and acting mercifully to show God how much we love Him is an expression of filial fear.

The fourth type of fear is worldly fear. It is unlike the first three fears because it is entirely evil. Earlier, we referred to this fear as a sin. Worldly fear is concerned with losing something or experiencing a punishment, and this fear convinces the person to turn against God. When faced with the choice between following God wholeheartedly and keeping or obtaining worldly goods, the person bound by worldly fear will compromise his morals. A person bound by worldly fear trusts

Good and Bad Fears

in the world, its goods, its benefits, and makes these things his end and goal. When these things fail him, he becomes fearful, despairing, and sad.

Worldly fear is the beginning of despair and causes a sense of hopelessness, whereas hope is the beginning of being daring. Despair proceeds from fear, just as fortitude, holy perseverance, proceeds from hope.[9] In other words, if we are to be daring conquerors of evil for Christ and in Christ, and boldly share His life-changing, soul-saving Gospel, we must conquer our fear of the devil, resist his threats, and boldly exercise hope in God that He will aid us in our efforts.

Timidity (an inordinate fear of any evil) is opposed to courage, fortitude, and perseverance. St. Paul exhorted his spiritual protégé, Timothy, that the Holy Spirit that lived within this young disciple was no cowardly Spirit (see 2 Tm 1:7). In other words, the Holy Spirit is not afraid of evil, and doesn't fear the loss of worldly benefits, but rather lives in us and helps us resist its threats as we strive to overcome the world. Indeed, "Whatever is born of God overcomes the world" (see 1 Jn 5:4).

One of the chief reasons why worldly fear is so insidious is that it removes us from the reality that we are sons of God the Father in Jesus Christ. It gradually conditions us to believe that we are alone, abandoned, and have no help. By living in fear we are no longer capable of living in right relationship with reality. We live in an unreal world of imaginary fears that are not rooted in God's truth.

Living in the fear of the future, also called forecasting by psychologists, can have debilitating effects and harmful consequences for your health, your freedom, your mental wellness, your relationships, and your self-confidence. Forecasting binds us in timidity and restrains us from living in the freedom of the Holy Spirit.

St. Thomas tells us, "It belongs to a brave man to expose himself to danger or death for the sake of the good. But to die to escape poverty, lust, or that which is disagreeable is cowardice.[10]" He continues, "It is natural for a man to shrink from detriment to his own body and loss of worldly goods, but to forsake justice on that account is contrary to reason." In other words, *to sin is far worse than to suffer.*

Test yourself. Where do you lack hope, perseverance, and courage? Do you lack perseverance in your marriage? Do you lack real hope in your occupation or your spiritual endeavors? Have you lost the courage to be a bold example of Christ's love? Determine the areas of your life where you lack hope and sense that discouragement and despair are taking over. It is precisely in those areas that the devil is instilling fear and attempting to rob you of the courage and fortitude needed to take the prudential risks that will enable you to forge, or reforge, relationships that will build the Kingdom of God.

3.

The Six Consequences of Fear

Perhaps you aren't yet convinced that F.E.A.R. is an underlying influence in much of your decision making, and that it has not had any real negative effects on your life's trajectory. F.E.A.R is subtle, and thus we can be dissuaded from the notion that it is a real factor that influences our decisions. Let's probe a little further and see if that is true. You may be surprised at how deeply F.E.A.R has embedded itself in your daily thinking.

Now that we understand the origin of fear, the types of fear that are good and those that are evil, let's understand the major effects of fear.

Before we proceed, it is important to mention that the consequences of fear are numerous and varied, and include anxiety, depression, retreating, alcoholism, nervous breakdowns, lack of self-confidence, ruptured relationships, and the like.

However, for our purposes, I will attempt to categorize the consequences of fear into six broad categories. The purpose is to help us identify where the cancer of fear has covertly lodged itself and is secretly metastasizing in our soul. If we stay the course, we will begin to see that fear is operating in the background and potentially

The Six Consequences of Fear

causing major *interfearence* in nearly every aspect of our lives.

If a doctor wants to heal his patient, it is imperative that he know his patient's ailment. The patient's symptoms indicate what type of illness he has. Once we, like the doctor, know the "symptoms," that is, the consequences of fear, we can begin to identify ways to overcome it.

The six major consequences of caving to worldly fear are 1) miserliness, 2) shame, 3) disobedience, 4) paralyzation of progress, 5) discouragement and despair, and ultimately 6) the suffocation of charity, making love grow cold. Let's examine each of these individually to determine if worldly fear is running *interfearence* in our lives.

Consequence #1: Miserliness

A miser is someone who is reluctant to spend money, sometimes to the point of forgoing basic comforts and perhaps some necessities, in order to hoard money or increasing his possessions. A prime example of a miser is Charles Dicken's Ebenezer Scrooge. Most of us don't hoard money in the way that Scrooge did. Yet, miserliness, like anything, has its levels of intensity.

If you are a miser or have the characteristic of being miserly at any level, it is a certain sign that worldly fear is a dominating force in your decision making. Miserliness undermines generosity. A generous person is ready to give more of his money, time, and talents than is necessary, required, or expected.

The generous person lavishly gives to the poor (see Ps 112:9). Generosity is one of the defining characteristics of a Christian. Christ Himself is the embodiment of generosity. He gave His time to healing lepers, the blind, and the sick. He fed the multitudes when they were hungry. He sacrificed His very own life to redeem us; He relieves us of our sinful debt by becoming sin for us (2 Cor 5:21), that we may live in communion with our Heavenly Father. To be a Christian is to be like Christ;, therefore a true Christian is generous, not miserly.

Our Lord, in His Sermon on the Mount, commands us to "Give and it will be given to you" (Lk 6:38). Notice that our Lord promises that being generous is always rewarded. Indeed, "A generous person will prosper; whoever refreshes others will be refreshed" (Prv 11:25). And "Good will come to those who are generous and lend freely, who conduct their affairs with justice" (Ps 112:5).

F.E.A.R., however, convinces us that the more we give the less we will have. When we believe this lie, we begin to think and act like a miser. Personally, I feel the tension between being actively generous and hoarding my resources on a weekly, if not daily basis.

For example, I recently became aware of a couple of larger expenditures that had to be paid within the next couple of weeks. "Not a problem," I thought, "I have it covered." The following Sunday, a parishioner from our church and I were having a conversation regarding his parents' and sibling's difficult situation in Africa. He lacked the financial resources to go to Congo and felt great sadness about his inability to be present and help them. I sensed that God was asking me to alleviate this man's concern. I calculated the cost in addition to the larger expenditures that needed to be paid and thought I could help. So I did.

The next week, the air-conditioner compressor in my wife's car stopped working. So we took it to the repair shop and paid for it to be replaced ($1500). A week later, the starter in my car broke. So we took it to the repair shop and paid for it to be replaced($450). Within days,

The Six Consequences of Fear

I received a letter from a global missions group indicating that the annual financial support for the children we had sponsored was due.

Often, when I decide to act in faith and be generous, all hell breaks loose. It is in situations like this that I am extremely tempted to pull back, temporarily withdrawing my support of the Church, my parish, and less fortunate children, and refusing to lend to those in need. Why? Because I become fearful of having less. I become afraid that I am losing my financial security.

When I am confronted with the opportunity to be generous, a multitude of doubts crash upon my finite faith. If I allow these doubts to gain ground in my mind, fear begins to grip me. Now, this fear is not the kind of fear that scares me, as a ghost or demon would. But it does instill an unsettling feeling in my soul. When this happens, I am tempted to react emotionally rather than logically.

My feelings and emotions become unruly and convince me to defend what is my own, what I have worked so hard to earn. My emotions influence me to ask questions like "Why should I give my hard-earned cash to someone who doesn't work?" Or think things like "He's not my responsibility. I have a wife and kids to provide for. Isn't that enough?"

Logic derived from divine wisdom, however, asks me, "In giving to God have you ever been outdone in generosity? Has there ever been a time when God has not supplied for your needs?" I think, "I've prayed 'Give us this day our daily bread' every day. I am nearly fifty years of age, and God has answered that prayer daily, three times a day—at least—totaling approximately fifty-five thousand answered prayers." God promises "give and it will be given to you. A good measure, pressed down, shaken together, and running over, will be poured into your lap. For the measure you give, it will be measured to you" (Lk 6:38).

During Christ's time on earth, people purchased and stored grain in burlap sacks. Jesus is describing what happens to the person who is generous: He is like a person who at harvest time is not in fields, but sitting down. Suddenly a harvest is thrown into his lap. He did very little to obtain it. Further, the grain is pressed down, shaken, which means that every nook and cranny of that sack is filled to the maximum. The sack is fat tight. In addition to this, our Lord promises that the grain will abundantly flow over and beyond the limit of the sack. This is a symbol of the reward that is given to the generous. This is divine logic.

Miserliness attacks our ability to think with the mind of Christ and to be generous. Miserliness is always born of F.E.A.R. The level to which we give to others generously is the level at which we are conquering our fears. In other words, giving generously to others is a certain way to overcome fear. The devil knows that if you are conquered by fear, you will not only give less, but live less, and have less—and so will others. More than that, he knows that when we lack generosity, souls are not converted to Christ's love. People come to know Christ not simply by people teaching about Christ, but through people who give and live like Christ.

While our third daughter, Anna Marie, was hospitalized and on life support, I lost my job. We were already scraping by, living below the poverty line. In addition to this, the hospital bills were piling up. We were defaulting on our gas and electric payments and having difficulty purchasing groceries and gas. Our situation was desperate if not nearing hopelessness.

The Six Consequences of Fear

While I was at the hospital with Anna Marie, a friend visited me, lent me his cell phone, and gave me $250 in cash. I was elated. During Anna Marie's hospitalization, I developed a friendship with a young couple whose daughter had contracted a disease that was literally eating her flesh. The father confided that they were dirt poor and were also struggling emotionally.

At that time I was praying continually, and it seemed that the power and confidence of God was guiding me. The day before Anna Marie was released from the hospital, I said goodbye to this young man and gave him the last of the money in my pocket. He was overcome with joy. I remember feeling like I was the one who'd won the lottery. I explained to him that the money was not mine, but given to me, and I was called to give it to him. Truly the Lord says it is better to give than to receive (see Acts 20:35).

After returning home, reality began to set in. I became overwhelmed by our pitiful financial situation. As I looked at our children, I began to wonder if giving that $200 away was a stupid idea. Then there was a knock at the front door. It was Greg, a friend from our church. He had with him a large manilla envelope and explained that members of our church were praying around the clock for our family. He went on to say that they were not only praying. Then he emptied the envelope onto our dining-room table. A mountain of cash fell out, thousands of dollars. Not only did that cash get us through some very challenging times, but it increased my faith and made me more aware of how much God cares for us.

Shortly after that, the children's hospital that saved Anna Marie's life waived our portion of the payment—approximately ninety thousand dollars. "Good measure, pressed down, shaken together, running over, will be poured [on your dining-room table]."

The point is this: don't let fear rob you of experiencing the glory of being generous and receiving the generosity of God. Miserliness is a sure sign that fear is directing your decisions. Don't let it. Be not afraid. God will never be outdone in generosity.

Consequence #2: Shame

Shame can be defined as a painful feeling of humiliation or distress caused by the consciousness of wrong or foolish behavior. While it is true that being caught in adultery, getting arrested, or your friends and family seeing a video of you drunk on Facebook can be the cause of shame, often we experience shame on a much deeper, personal level. It's one thing to be ashamed of our actions; it is another thing altogether to be ashamed of who we are. Being ashamed of ourselves, our bodies, our personality, our abilities, or lack thereof can all be the cause of incredible personal pain.

In junior high, it was mandatory to take showers at the end of gym class. Being a naked sixth-grade boy who showered with the seventh- and eighth-grade guys instilled in me a certain fear of inadequacy. The fear began with a doubt: I haven't matured like the other guys. I'm not a man yet. The doubt created an emotional anxiety that allowed fear to overcome me. I would try to skip showering or to skip gym class. But logic, if I had listened, was telling me that I could not help who I was, or the rate at which my body was maturing. Nevertheless, personal shame—for being me—was a result of a deep-seated fear.

People feeling embarrassed about public speaking, or undressing in front of their spouse, or showing themselves in public after losing their hair due to chemotherapy, or simply feeling as though they can't compare to others, are examples of personal shame that is born from fear.

Shame attacks and undermines the human person's God-given dignity. The devil uses this shame as a way to intimidate you, to get you to back off, and not believe that you are a child of God. God, on the other hand, desires that you become a living manifestation, a revelation of His glory. The evil one constantly attempts to intimidate us with shame, hoping that we will cover up our true glory. If the evil one succeeds, those around you may never come to know the love and power of Jesus Christ that was intended to flow through you and into them.

On a good day, my height measures at a whopping five foot seven. I'm short. Being short isn't so bad . . .

when you are alone. But when I'm standing in a circle of taller men, which happens very often, I am tempted to feel insecure. I've never liked looking up other people's nostrils, and I like even less when people look down on me. It's tempting to avoid socializing because I don't enjoy feeling small. Yet God calls me to rejoice, be thankful and confident in the person He has created me to be. After all, it wasn't my choice to be short—it was His—and I can't do anything to change that reality.

Logic tells me that God loves to demonstrate His strength in our weaknesses (see 2 Cor 12:8). When I consider the people who I most admire and who had the most profound impact on my life, none of them were supermodels, wealthy, great-looking, or had superhuman exterior qualities and talents. In fact, most of them, from the outside, appeared to be ordinary, not overly attractive, and sometimes sickly looking. These

The Six Consequences of Fear

people would have been in the class of Mother Teresa both in looks and in love.

It is easy for us to believe that we need to appear sleek and strong to change the world and win it for Christ. But God doesn't say that His glory is manifest in our sleekness, but in our weakness.

Whether you are ashamed of your weight, your thinning hair, the abnormal bump on your forehead, your height, your inability to speak eloquently, or your failure to perform under pressure, it is important that you understand that the devil wants you to doubt your God-given goodness and avoid injecting yourself into the lives of others.

Consider that Moses, after being called by God to lead the Israelites, was reluctant to fulfill his God-given mission because he had a speech impediment. Yet, he was the man whom God chose to liberate His people.

God relishes manifesting His glory in our weakness. He loves blowing people's stereotypes and preconditioned mind-sets out of the water.

Three years ago we moved into a house surrounded by woods. I quickly discovered that if I were to survive, I needed a chain saw. Up to that point in my life, I had used a chain saw only a handful of times. During my first week of using my new chain saw, it would start, run, and then die. Sometimes I could get it started, other times I couldn't. It seemed to be malfunctioning consistently and for no apparent reason. I called the hardware store where I purchased it and explained that I had a "dud." My new chain saw had a manufacturer defect and needed to be replaced. Kindly, they invited me to bring it in and they would look at it.

The following morning I arrived at the hardware store wearing a white short-sleeve polo shirt and a freshly

The Six Consequences of Fear

pressed pair of tan dress slacks, and my "malfunctioning" chain saw in hand. As I set the chain saw on the reception desk, a young, red-haired, fair-skinned gal appeared from behind the workbench, where she was repairing a small engine. The smudges of grease under both of her eyes made her look like she was an offensive wide receiver. Her fingernails were short, and utterly caked with grime. Insecurity set in. I actually considered leaving or making a lame excuse like "my friend asked me to drop this off for him." Breaking my escapist thoughts she asked, "Are you the guy who called yesterday about the new chain saw not working?" I nodded.

After explaining the situation to her, she responded, "Show me how *you* start it." I began to sweat . . . all over. Talk about performance anxiety. As it turned out, I wasn't starting my chain saw properly, and because of this I was flooding the engine. Shame invaded every atom of my being. It was in that moment that I made an intentional choice to stop pretending that I was "the man" who had purchased a bum chain saw and learn from this young lady how to use the blessed power tool.

Because of her, I now have confidence when I fell trees. In fact, by humbling myself, I upheld her dignity and affirmed her talents. She actually laughed as I said while leaving, "Thanks for helping this yuppy city boy."

Are you afraid, ashamed to be yourself? Are you humiliated and ashamed by what you don't know? Are you ashamed of your personality, your beliefs, the way you look, the way you laugh, your inexperience? Many of us, in one way or another, are ashamed of certain aspects of ourselves, which means that most of us are continually being gnawed at by fear.

The key to overcoming shame induced by fear is to believe and trust that God knows what He is doing and why He created you the way He created you. It is not necessary that you know why, but that you trust that God does. As St. Catherine of Siena said, "Become who you are and set the world ablaze." When we become who we are, who God has intended us to be, there is no cause for fear or shame. St. Paul asks, "Am I trying to please people? If I were still trying to please people, I would not be Christ's servant" (Gal 1:10). A true servant of Christ is powerful and effective, overcoming fear because he cares very little about comparisons and human assessment. The servant of Christ knows that he is a child of God and that identity determines everything.

Consequence #3: Paralyzation of Progress

Newton's first law of motion is that an object in motion stays in motion, while an object at rest remains at rest.

This law applies not only to physics, but also to the spiritual life.

Progress is essential in the spiritual life. If you are not ascending you are descending. Self-helpers contend that happiness is derived from progress. The type of progress they refer to is being physically strong, increasing your intellectual capacity, amassing wealth, defying age, decreasing your body fat and wrinkles, and growing your fan base. Unfortunately, the laws of physics and human experience teach us that somewhere around the age of fifty, the human body stops progressing toward a pinnacle ideal, but rather begins to atrophy and descend down the bell curve of "progress."

Which raises the question: how can a person, even when he seems to be falling apart physically, continue to progress? The ideal of human progress is actually subjective. It is based on what a person is progressing toward.

The Six Consequences of Fear

If point B is your goal and you are moving further from point A and closer to point B, that is considered progress. However, everyone has a different version of point B. Further, every person's starting point—his genetic code—is different. The self-helper's message regarding progress is convincing because it speaks of achieving an ideal self. However, by default self-helpers cannot help but to teach us to compare ourselves to them and to others. They condition us to believe that everyone has the same point B. The Christian progresses toward Christ, his North Star, which is communion with God and eternal glory in heaven. Every Christian has the same point A—fallen human nature that is debilitated by original sin; and every Christian has the same point B: Christ and communion with His Father.

The "gospel" of the self-help guru ultimately fails when their protégé's health fails or his death is imminent. A

Christian, however, can progress, grow, and achieve great things even when he is bedridden and dying.

It is crucial that we understand and believe this proposal. Why? Because this truth inspires us to press on toward achieving our goals in spite of the most alarming fears.

When the self-helper becomes ill or impaired, suffers financial loss, or is diagnosed with a terminal illness, self-improvement is off the table and put perpetually on hold. His life is reduced to a struggle for survival. When the Christian encounters hardship, he discovers the divine paradox of Christ's power being manifest in his weakness. Consider that while Jesus died on the Cross, He transformed that Cross into a pulpit. His words still echo in man's hearts to this very day: "Father, forgive them for they know not what they do" (Lk 23:34). Even to the bitter end, Jesus is progressing toward a goal.

The Six Consequences of Fear

A Christian does not fear death because divine logic tells him that death is a step in the progression toward eternal communion with God. People fear death because they are more afraid of losing earthly possessions than they are longing for God. They are fearful of God because they love their possessions more than they love Him.

To modify the prayer of St. Francis of Assisi, "In giving we receive, in pardoning we are pardoned, in dying we are born to eternal life, and in failing we learn to succeed."

People often interpret fear of failure as they do death. It is the end. Like the fear of death, fear of failure can be a most definite way to paralyze real progress in all aspects of our lives.

Many of us fear failing because on a deeper level we fear the loss of our self-inflated identity. We think we are better than we really are, and therefore we resist facing those challenges that confront us with the reality that we are less than we think ourselves to be.

Failures are essential to becoming successful. Success is not defined by an absence of failure. Success is only obtained by failing and learning from the failure why you failed. It is obtained by trying again with an approach that doesn't make the same mistakes, and then developing an approach that is better than the previous ones. It has been said that success is going from one failure to another with great enthusiasm. This enthusiasm is derived from the hope that we will eventually learn how to succeed.

If we believe that success is an absence of failure, we will remain bound in fear of failure, and that fear will paralyze all forms of progress, and we will never become who we are intended to be or do what we have been called by God to do.

The Six Consequences of Fear

There once was a man who lost his job in 1832, was defeated for state legislature in 1832, failed in business in 1833, and was finally elected to state legislature in 1834. His sweetheart died in 1835, he had nervous breakdown in 1836. He was defeated for Speaker of the House in 1838, and was defeated for nomination for Congress in 1843. He was finally elected to Congress in 1846 but lost renomination in 1848. He was rejected for land officer in 1849, defeated for U.S. Senate in 1854, was defeated for nomination for vice president in 1856, and was again defeated for U.S. Senate in 1858. He was elected president in 1860. This man was one of the greatest presidents in the history of the United States: Abraham Lincoln.[11]

Lincoln's example teaches us that failures, if learned from, can lead to great success. But most of us either quit after our first failure, or worse, quit before we begin. Successful YouTubers say that the biggest reason why people fail to launch a successful YouTube channel is because they are afraid and delay posting their first video. The trap of perfectionism is a major component of the fear of failure. Whether you are writing a manuscript, remodeling your kitchen, painting a portrait, rewiring your electrical, beginning to train with a fitness coach, launching a business venture or the like, you can be certain that a big part of your reason for postponing your efforts is due to the fear of failure, and also, at times, its evil younger stepsister perfectionism, and these fears will consistently paralyze your progress.

Perfectionism is rooted in the fear of being critiqued, receiving critical feedback, or being evaluated negatively. We want whatever we do to be perfect, without error, so that we can avoid someone bashing what we

The Six Consequences of Fear

produce. We don't want someone to burst our self-inflated egotistical bubble.

When I wrote my first manuscript, I was afraid of sharing it with our writers group. I was not a writer, but I had a wee little hope that I could aspire to be a writer. I didn't have a clue. At that time, I didn't know when to use a comma or a semicolon (I still don't). I didn't use paragraphs (can you imagine?). Past tense, present tense, future tense, made no sense. By continually and persistently overcoming my fear of failure, the guys gave me critical feedback, which often included affirmation regarding the actual content.

After nearly five years of sharing my writings with them, the very, very rough manuscript, which had become four volumes, was completed. Fearful of sending it to an editor, I asked my friend Joe, who is a writing phenom, if he would edit the book. Joe's edits confirmed one thing: that I was not a writer. After receiving the edited file from Joe, I opened it reluctantly and stared at the screen in horror. It looked like it had been caught in a drive-by shooting. Red was all over the place. My initial reaction was to shut down the file and never write again.

But I took a deep breath and went through each edit and comment one by one, and eventually overcame my fear of failing at writing. The process was grueling and grinding and painful for both Joe and me (remarkably, we are still friends to this very day).

After the manuscript was finalized, I wanted to share it with friends, but was fearful that people would reject it. Nevertheless, I worked up the courage to send a hard copy to a number of people, including a friend who happened to personally know a publicist who was working with a prominent worldwide Catholic book publisher. Without me knowing, he sent the manuscript to the publicist, who shared it with the publisher, who contacted me asking if they could publish the book, which eventually became one of their bestsellers.

If at any point I had allowed my fear of failure, which was constantly hammering at me, to convince me that I was not a writer, my first book would never have been published nor my second, nor my fifteenth.

The key is humility and trust in God. We are, as St. Peter admonishes us, to "be humbled therefore under the mighty hand of God, that he may exalt you in due time" (1 Pt 5:6). If we are humble enough to embrace our failures and learn from them, while trusting that "God will see the good work that He has begun in us unto completion" (see Phil 1:6) we will eventually experience personal victories and successes.

What is it that God is calling you to do? What is that desire that He has placed in your heart? Will you act upon that God-given desire with faith in Him? How does He want you to be Christ to others? If fear is causing *interfearence* in your mission, commit yourself to taking that next small step, even if it means a certain failure, that you may learn from your mistakes and eventually rise in victory over your fears. Newton's first law of motion can be adapted for the Christian: A Christian who does nothing will eventually be nothing. But a Christian that is moved by God and moves for God will move others toward God.

Consequence #4: Avoidance of Risk

Risk. The word sounds dangerous. Because that is the essence of risk. Risk can be defined as exposing yourself, or something you value, to danger, harm, or loss.

The Six Consequences of Fear

Here we encounter the reoccurring theme of loss head-on. Risk is only risky, only dangerous, if a potential loss of something or someone is involved.

On the flip side of risk is glorious achievement. We often hail those people who risked everything, including themselves, for a greater mission.

For example, Clemens August Graf von Galen, a Catholic bishop, lived in Munster, Germany, during the rise of Hitler and the Nazi regime. Bishop von Galen spoke openly and boldly regarding his disdain for Nazi racism and totalitarianism. In fact, von Galen sent his complaints directly to Hitler himself, and when he did not receive a response from him, he resorted to using the pulpit to protest the Nazis and their mandate that all crucifixes be removed from school. Von Galen rallied a protest large enough that Hitler allowed the crucifixes to remain in the schools.

InterFEARence

According to Stephanie Hertzenberg, "Von Galen was perhaps best known for his vehement opposition to Hitler's euthanasia program. In a series of fiery sermons, von Galen decried the program and warned that the Nazis could use the program to dispose of anyone they disliked. Von Galen's sermon on August 3, 1941, is his best known today. The sermon was powerful and persuasive enough that anti-Nazi forces circulated it throughout Germany, and Allied planes dropped leaflet copies of the sermon on German cities. Nazi officials demanded that von Galen be executed, but Joseph Goebbels feared that making a martyr of von Galen would galvanize the sizable Catholic population and lend credence to von Galen's anti-Nazi claims. They decided to wait to kill von Galen until after the end of World War II. Von Galen was made a cardinal by Pope Pius XII for his 'fearless resistance' against Hitler."[12]

The Six Consequences of Fear

Von Galen overcame Hitler's intimidations, and because he risked everything, including his own life, he became an image of hope to the German resistance.

The evil one will attempt to convince us that to risk for Christ will cost us comfort, security, and safety. And it will. But more precisely, the evil one will attempt to convince us that it is impossible to live without these things. Comfort, security, and safety are good and necessary and from God. Indeed, if life is one continual risk, we would certainly die of anxiety, mental illness, or a heart attack—or all of the above.

But what happens when our efforts to maintain our own comfort, security, and safety becomes a primary factor in our decision making? Eventually we refrain from risking our health, our financial resources, or our honor for the purpose of helping others because it could cause us to be uncomfortable or unsafe.

InterFEARence

What if you never risked the discomfort of rejection and instead neglected to ask the woman you were destined to marry on a date? You would not be married—at least to her. What if you decided to remain comfortable and not have children? You would never experience the joy of having your own family, not to mention the joy of grandchildren. What if you never went to college for fear of going into debt? You most likely would not have the job you have today.

When we fearfully avoid prudential risk, we become ineffective, which greatly reduces our ability to provide life, hope, and a better future to others. Recently a friend from Ireland sent a newspaper article about an Italian pastor that exemplifies the incredible hope one person can give by risking his life. The article reads:

"Not even in my darkest nightmares did I imagine I would see and live that which is happening here

The Six Consequences of Fear

in our hospital for the past three weeks. The nightmare continues, the river always becomes bigger. At the beginning some people arrived, then tens, then hundreds, and now we are no longer doctors but we have become like factory workers sorting on the conveyor belt and we decide who lives and who should be sent home to die, even if all of these people have paid their taxes to Italy their entire life. Up until two weeks ago, my colleagues and I were atheists; it was normal because we are doctors and have learned that science excludes the presence of God. I always laughed at my parents who used to go to church.

"Nine days ago, a seventy-five-year-old pastor came to us. He was a gentle man; he had very serious respiratory problems, but he carried a Bible with him. He impressed us because he read to the dying and would hold their hand.

"All of us doctors were tired, discouraged, psychologically and physically done, when we had the time [we would] listen to him.

"Now we have to admit that we as humans have reached our limit, we cannot do any more and more people die every day. We are exhausted. Two of our colleagues have died and others have been infected.

"We realize that whatever man is able to do ends, then we need God and we started to ask Him for help. When we have a few free minutes, we speak amongst ourselves and we cannot believe that, from being ferocious atheists, we are now in search of our peace every day, asking the Lord to help us resist so that we can continue to care for the sick. Yesterday the seventy-five-year-old pastor died, and until today, despite having another 120 deaths in three weeks here and us all being completely exhausted and destroyed, he managed,

The Six Consequences of Fear

despite his condition and difficulties, to bring peace which we no longer hoped to find.

The pastor went home to the Lord and soon we will also follow him if it continues like this. I haven't been home in six days and I don't know when I ate last and I realize my uselessness on this earth, and I want to dedicate my last breath to helping others. I am happy to have returned to God while I am surrounded by the suffering and death of my fellow men."[13]

If it wasn't' for this pastor ministering to Italian Covid patients, or the likes of St. Peter and St. Paul, or St. Maximilian Kolbe substituting himself for a father who was selected by the Nazis to be executed, and the multitude of faithful witnesses that we call saints, many of us would not have faith in Jesus Christ or the eternal salvation that He has won for us.

We may not be called to the heroism of the martyrs,

but we can overcome our fear of rejection and failure and take minimal, prudential risks for Christ daily. Those who take these risks are the modern saints through whom Christ's light shines into the darkness of man's lost soul.

Years ago I took my daughter to a local coffee shop for a date and noticed a small family sitting at another table. Having recently started a Catholic ministry for fathers, I was inspired to give the dad of the family one of our cards with the times and dates of our men's group meetings. Fear suddenly set in. What if he laughs, rejects me, or ignores me? What if he is a Catholic hater? Nevertheless, I overcame my fear of rejection and introduced myself. He received the card graciously and silently smiled when I invited him to our next meeting.

Several weeks later, Andy, the man to whom I gave the card, showed up at our Wednesday morning gathering.

Andy has continued to attend for the last six years. I gained a friendship, and Andy gained a community of friends and an awakening of his faith in Jesus Christ. Today his family is on fire with the love of God.

Perhaps most of us fear rejection because no one is overcoming *their* fear of rejection and reaching out to us. When people dare to share God's love with us, their example inspires us to go and do likewise. You and I can be the modern-day saints, the Abraham Lincolns, the von Galens, who conquer our fear of failure and rejection and daringly risk ourselves to bring the message of Christ's love to others.

Consequence #5: Discouragement That Leads to Despair

Since surrendering my life to Jesus Christ at the age of twenty-four, the desire to serve Him had become increasingly intense. During the decade following my conversion, on occasion people I knew and didn't know would tell me that I should consider becoming a deacon.

Somewhere in my mid-thirties, our diocese reinstated the diaconate program. I understood this as a sign from God that I should apply. After completing the application, the interviews with the formation director, and the psychiatrist, and taking the psychological personality tests, I was accepted into the program.

Over time, I had become friends with the formation director. We would occasionally go out for coffee and talk shop. Toward the end of my first year of aspirancy, my wife and I were scheduled for an informal "meet and greet" with the bishop and the formation director. This was standard protocol for all of the diaconate candidates. After we arrived at the diocesan headquarters for our "informal" meeting, my wife was asked to wait in a

The Six Consequences of Fear

separate room while I was escorted to another room to meet privately with the bishop and the director. I felt uneasy. Something wasn't right.

The meeting began with the formation director introducing me to the bishop as though he had no personal relationship with me. It felt incredibly awkward. He proceeded to talk to the bishop about me as though I was not present, explaining that I had failed the psychological evaluation (which I took to enter the program).

He told the bishop that I could be a potential problem for the Church, that I was unfit for ministry, and he recommended that I undergo serious ongoing psychological counseling. Then turning to me, he said that if I wanted to remain in the program, I would have to attend biweekly counseling sessions with a psychiatrist of their choosing, and I would have to pay for it. After a year they would determine my psychological status and whether I could proceed in the diaconate program. As we ended the session, he concluded by saying, "Oh, and please don't share this information with anyone. People may get the wrong impression about you and we wouldn't want that."

My head was spinning. "What is inside me?" I thought. "Could I be that bad? What just happened?" My hopes to serve Christ and His Church appeared to be being sabotaged by this one man. What occurred afterward was more painful than the meeting itself.

The obstacles that had arisen led to a host of self-doubts, including the doubt of my calling, the questioning of my identity, and the perplexing ways of God.

The doubts came with associated fears: Is God rejecting me? Am I not good enough to serve God's people? What do they see in me that I don't? Will I ever have an opportunity to serve God?

The Six Consequences of Fear

These fears gave way to serious, debilitating discouragement. Though my spiritual director recommended that I "stay and fight" and remain resolute in my calling, I began to lack the strength, resilience, and courage to persevere. The feeling of discouragement, which attacked my ability to be courageous, left me feeling weak, disheartened, ineffective, unmotivated, and powerless.

These feelings began to condition what I believed about myself. I spiraled into serial self-deprecation, believing that I was a failure, not good enough, lacking what it takes, and that God did not need me and that I could not make a real difference in anyone's life.

To attempt to offset my terribly distorted, negative self-image, I would try to overcompensate in the opposite direction. Often these acts of overcompensation would lead to acts of disobeying God. I felt weak, so I would posture as though I were strong, which led to me being perceived as prideful (which I was). I felt stupid, so I would try to appear smart, which led to many arguments. I felt isolated, so I would look for inclusion in disordered ways, eventually getting on people's nerves.

If I had not responded to the Holy Spirit's promptings of hope, I would eventually have despaired, lost my faith, and eventually lost my soul.

I share this account to reveal a grave consequence of fear, which I call the 6 D's. If unchecked, the 6 D's will D-rail you from being an effective, bold, risk-taking, loving disciple of Jesus Christ.

So how does the D-railing process of the 6 D's unfold? It begins with you having a goal. The goal could be big or small. As you work confidently toward achieving your goal, obstacles arise. Some of the obstacles are minor. But if there are enough of them, they can become a mountain that seems insurmountable. If a larger obstacle is added to that load, it could be the straw that breaks the camel of confidence's back.

If we respond to these obstacles emotionally rather than logically, we will become highly vulnerable to ***doubt*** (D-1). We begin doubting the goal. We think, "Maybe it was a stupid idea to begin with." We begin to doubt our calling: maybe I misunderstood God. "Was I imagining that I was called?" We begin to doubt God: maybe He doesn't care; maybe He isn't real. When doubt takes hold of us, we begin to remove our eyes from Christ and reject His power and plan. Remember Peter walking on the water: when he began to doubt, he realized that he could not stand or float on his own power.

At this point we can only see the waves of doubt, and because of this we become ***discouraged*** (D-2). This discouragement is an attack against courage, the fortitude that is necessary to proceed with the calling we have received from God.

If we become discouraged enough, we will begin to evaluate ourselves negatively, believing that we lack strength, courage, honor, and fortitude. We forget that God, the Holy Spirit, dwells in us and can do the impossible through us.

This eventually leads to serial self-***deprecation*** (D-3) of self. Self-deprecation fosters deep self-hatred. The evil one offers you a deceptive view of yourself. He attempts to separate your identity from God who dwells in you. He whispers into your soul, "You are a failure. No one needs you. You will make no real difference in anyone's life. Stop wasting your time. No one will notice if you are gone. You can't do anything right. You are a loser."

The Six Consequences of Fear

If we listen to his voice, we will begin to repeat his deceptions; and repeating his lies, we brainwash ourselves into believing in his distorted view of us.

When we self-deprecate, we actually depreciate our perception of our personal value and fail to see or understand how God values us and loves us. At this point, we are stepping outside of faith in God and His power. God warns us, "Without faith it is impossible to please God" (Heb 11:6). It is imperative that we understand this point. Many people who reach this level of self-loathing believe that God has abandoned them. The reality is that they have abandoned faith in God. They refuse to believe that God loves them, has a plan for them, and will come to their aid. They believe that they are beyond hope.

The human person cannot remain perpetually in a state of self-loathing. We feel the need to do something to offset the terrible feelings we have about ourselves and will do nearly anything to feel better about our self-image. This explains why the man who feels weak and unattractive falls prey to viewing porn. He uses a woman who cannot reject him. This grants him a fleeting, momentary feeling of false strength. This explains why people who feel depressed, or "down," take an upper, or even a downer like alcohol. We use stimulants and depressants to change our disposition because we lack the peace of Christ. More commonly, people often overeat and overdrink, video binge-watch, and squander their bodies and time because they are looking for something that will give them consolation rather than the Consoler who alone can feed them with divine life.

After we awake from the stupor of self-indulgent sin, the evil one rubs our noses in our sinful poop of **disobedience** (D-4). He convincingly condemns us: "You're

The Six Consequences of Fear

pathetic. Look at you. You call yourself a Christian. You aren't a Christian—you're Judas. You are a betrayer. How could He ever forgive you? It would be better had you not been born. He laid down His very life for you, and you spit in His face."

People who have hit this low are left with two options: repent and believe in God the Father's willingness to forgive, and that His mercy is endless; or ***despair*** (D-5) either by killing themselves, or forgoing a relationship with Christ and proceeding headlong into an addiction to sin.

By choosing the latter option, the evil one has moved that person from the realm of despair to spiritual ***death*** (D-6). Doubt, discouragement, deprecation, disobedience, and despair ultimately lead to death of the soul. This is the process of the satanic D-railing of our faith and the consequence of bowing down to worldly fear.

What is the remedy? How can we be set free from this vicious cycle? The way is simple to comprehend but perhaps the most difficult thing to do: trust God even when it looks hopeless.

Later, I will share how God saved me from discouragement and despair, thus fulfilling my God-given desire to serve Him, despite being rejected by those who supposedly represented Him. I know from personal experience, and can promise you, that the Lord will never forsake those who seek Him (see Ps 9:10) . . . and trust Him.

Consequence #6: Suffocation of Charity

When Jesus was questioned by a scribe: who is my neighbor? Jesus responded to his question with the incredible parable of the Good Samaritan. The scribe was really asking Jesus, "Are there any restrictions as to whom I extend my help and forgiveness?"

The Six Consequences of Fear

In this parable, our Lord describes a man who was traveling from Jerusalem to Jericho and fell among brigands who stripped him, laid blows upon him, and went away leaving him half-dead (see Lk 10:25-37). Jesus mentions three other characters in this account: a priest, a Levite, and a Samaritan. The priest looks at the man lying on the side of the road but remains on the other side and passes by. The priest was certainly concerned with the law that stated that if any man touches a dead body, he was unclean for seven days (Num 19:11). He feared that the man lying on the side of the road was dead and convinced of this he chose not to touch him lest he lose his turn to serve in the Temple. In other words, he feared spiritual defilement.

The second character is a Levite who also passes by. Because "the road to Jericho from Jerusalem [has] rocky passages and sudden turns, it [was] an ideal place for brigands to kill people. In the fifth century Jerome tells us that it was still called The Red, or Bloody Way . . . As late as the early 1930s the travel writer H. V. Morton tells us that he was warned to get home before dark, if he intended to use the road because a certain Abu Jildah was adept at holding up cars and robbing travelers and tourists and escaping to the hills before the police could arrive."[14] This was the same road from Jerusalem to Jericho that Jesus was referring to.

Often bandits would use decoys, such as a supposed injured person, to lure people for the purpose of robbing them. The Levite most likely is a representative of the self-protector who refrains from helping another because of his fear of personal injury.

The Samaritan, who stopped to help the man, was a foreigner to the Jew. To the Jew a Samaritan was a heretic who bastardized the religion of the Jews by worshipping

The Six Consequences of Fear

foreign gods. The hatred between Samaritans and Jews can be likened to the hatred between Christians and Muslims during the Crusades.

Yet, our Lord says that the Samaritan, the "enemy," is the one who broke cultural barriers in order to extend charity to the man who was half dead. The Samaritan, the one who Jews demonize as the devil himself, is the one who overcomes the fears that the priest and Levite could not.

The entire parable is an outgrowth of the scribe's initial question to Jesus: what is the greatest commandment? To which Jesus responds: love God and love your neighbor. The parable is meant to disclose two very prevalent fears that suffocate charity in a man's heart: the fear of spiritual contamination and the fear of being unprotected.

The first is religious elitism, an excuse to disassociate with those who are defiled by sin, or those who don't worship in the superior way that we do. Eventually this can become the fear of spiritual contamination. When we become afraid of spiritual defilement, we lock ourselves up in the "perfect" liturgy, or the "perfect" community. We make every effort to avoid sinners, or those of different sects or creeds, and protect ourselves behind the gates of religion. Because we protect ourselves, we fail to inject ourselves and Christ into others' lives. When we live in fear of being defiled by others, we no longer believe that a little divine light has the power to shine brightly in the darkness and overcome the kingdom of sin.

Our Lord did not say to Peter, "You are rock and upon this rock I will build my Church and hell will not prevail against its gates." But quite often that is how we interpret the meaning of Jesus' words, "The gates of Hell will not prevail against my church." My friend

The Six Consequences of Fear

David says, "Gates are created to defend that which is inside of those gates, and to keep people in . . . gates are not a weapon used in an offensive attack." When we succumb to the fear of spiritual contamination, we become fearful of losing our holiness. When we believe that our holiness hangs by a spiritual thread, we cannot be bold for Christ. We simply lock ourselves up behind our religious gates and cover up that spiritual thread, making sure that nothing sharp comes near it.

But Christ calls us to penetrate the gates of hell and bring His presence into the soul bound by the devil. The fear of spiritual contamination snuffs charity and our willingness to break open the gates of hell and deliver those imprisoned by the devil's blindness. Like the priest and the Levite in Jesus' parable, the person who is afraid of spiritual contamination abandons the soul in need out of self-protection.

InterFEARence

Fr. Damien of Molokai was a Catholic priest who was assigned to a quarantined community of lepers on the Hawaiian island of Molokai from 1873 until his death in 1889–an assignment that he greatly desired and pleaded for.

During his time of service to the lepers, he spearheaded the establishment of houses, school, roads, hospitals, and churches. He ate with the lepers, shared food, and even shared his smoking pipe with them.

During his homilies he would address the lepers as "you lepers," until after eleven years of caring for the physical, spiritual, and emotional needs of those in the leper colony he contracted the disease. After he discovered that he had leprosy, his next homily began with the words, "My fellow lepers."

Fr. Damien, heralded as a "Master of Charity," broke through the barriers of self-protection and fear and became "one" with the lepers. Love always associates itself with those who are unloved, that they may be loved.

The man left half dead on the side of the road to Jericho is a symbol of Adam and all of his descendants, who after leaving Jerusalem, a symbol of paradise, fell prey to brigands, a symbol of the devil, who has plundered our spiritual goods, leaving us all but spiritually dead. Christ is the Good Samaritan who leaves heaven and overcomes all forms of religious elitism, self-protection, and fear of spiritual contamination, and binds our sinful wounds with the wine and oil of the sacraments, including the forgiveness of our sins. He leaves us with the innkeeper, a symbol of the Church, whose duty it is to care for us and heal us.

Even two thousand years after His earthly ministry, Christ continues to pour His perfection into us sinful, marred, imperfect beings by feeding us with His body and blood in the most Holy Sacrament of the Eucharist.

Imagine if Fr. Damien allowed fear to restrain him from loving the lepers. Imagine if Christ, as He agonized in the garden of Gethsemane, caved in to fear and refused to proceed with His sacrifice on Mount Calvary? Where would we be? Imagine if you allow fear to restrain you from reaching out to those who are diseased bodily and spiritually. Where will they be without you and Christ who you are commissioned to bring to them?

4.

Conquering F.E.A.R. with R.I.S.K.

Certainly, it is helpful, if not vital, that we understand what F.E.A.R. is, how it originates in us, and the devastating limitations it imposes upon us. But just as crucial is having a strategy to conquer F.E.A.R. It is pointless to visit a doctor who diagnoses you with an illness but neglects to provide you with a healing remedy. So far, we've diagnosed the problem of F.E.A.R, but now it is time to provide a remedy for it.

As we have seen, F.E.A.R. if left unchecked can wreak major *interfearence* on nearly every aspect of our lives, leading to discouragement and ultimately despair, miserliness, personal shame for who we are, disobedience to God's inspirations, paralyzation of any real progress, a stunting of our willingness to risk and to be daring for Christ, and ultimately, the snuffing of charity, making our love grow cold.

What then can we do to shut down the *interfearence* that F.E.A.R. causes and begin to live the life God wills for us? The answer to that question is R.I.S.K., a simple, doable method that will help us not only identify our fears, but understand them clearly and have the power to conquer them consistently.

R.I.S.K. is a four-step process:

R: ***Recognize*** your fear.

I: ***Identify*** the source of your fear.

S: ***Surrender*** your fear to God.

K: ***Kindle*** trust in God by taking small risks.

Though the above schematic is self-explanatory, it will be beneficial to briefly describe each step.

R: Recognize Your Fear

Often our feelings take on disordered proportions. We become exceedingly angry, vengeful, overly disheartened, worried, and anxious. We stew about a particular situation without ever actually pausing and reflecting on why we our losing our grip on peace in Christ.

While running late for an appointment, have you ever found yourself stuck in traffic? Did your negative emotions escalate? Most of us have experienced this on many occasions. At the point when you sense that your emotions are overriding your ability to be reasonable, it is necessary to pause and accept the fact that you have become afraid. After you have accepted that reality, then you can proceed to the next step. Ask yourself, "Why am I afraid?"

Three years ago, my wife and I purchased our second home. The first day of ownership I moved all of our boxed possessions into the basement of the house. My wife planned on stopping by later that evening. We decided to do some minor work to the new home while we lived in our original home for the next couple of weeks. When she arrived, I had demolished several walls and a substantial amount of the main floor. I bit off far more than I could chew. I'm amazed that she did not divorce me.

To purchase the new house without having sold our old home, we obtained a balloon loan, a type of loan that does not fully amortize over its term. A balloon payment is required at the end of the term to repay the principal balance of the loan. In other words, at the end of five years I would a) have to pay the balance of my loan in full; b) sell the home to pay the loan off; c) refinance and obtain a new loan at the interest rate available, which could be significantly higher and could inflate our monthly payments beyond what we could afford; or d) be foreclosed on and lose the house, my investment, and perhaps my wife and kids.

The "remodel" became a complete overhaul. I gutted nearly every part of the house. The money from the sale of our previous home was applied to the new loan to bring down the principal. Over the course of the next year and half the remodeling project was rapidly depleting the money left in savings. At one point, I realized that we weren't halfway through the renovation process and did not have enough money to complete it. In addition, we encountered significant problems—such as piles of rodent carcasses in the old stud pockets of the kitchen, which indicated that we had a long-standing mouse infestation, as well as a bat infestation in the attics of the garage and the house. Even the hardwood floors contracted, gapped, and warped after installation. It seemed as though every day brought with it a new surprise with additional costs that we could not afford.

I began to fear that interest rates would skyrocket and felt pressured to get the house refinanced as soon as possible while rates were low. To do that, however, meant that at least 80 percent of the remodel had to be complete. I was stuck. I needed money to complete the remodel and refinance, but could not refinance because I didn't have enough cash to complete the project.

Moreover, if a contractor did his job well went up. And if a contractor did his job poorly (which happened a couple of times), he bailed, and I was left with a remodel of a remodel gone bad.

Over the course of the first year that we lived in our new home I exuded nearly every negative emotion on a daily basis. My wife went from being elated about the move to wishing we had never set eyes on the place.

Fear gripped me, and my inability to step back and think logically wreaked havoc in every aspect of my life, straining my marriage, stressing my relationship with my children, and sapping my determination to focus and perform well at work. I wore out my friends with my constant complaining.

Finally, during one of my rants about the house, a good friend interjected, "It's time to put the big boy pants on Devin." Ouch. Internally, I was fuming. How dare he accuse me of not being a man! But he was right. Too right. Fear had overtaken me, discouraging me, and debilitating my ability to think calmly and press forward in confidence.

For the first time in nearly a year, I paused and considered my situation logically. I spoke with my loan officer, who happened to be the friend who told me to put on the big-boy pants, and discussed the situation reasonably. He asked questions like: What is the minimum that needs to be completed to refinance and avoid foreclosure? How many of those projects could I do myself? He assured me that interest rates would remain under a certain percent and that there was nothing to fear.

Each day I prayed to God, asking Him to show me the *one* thing that I could work on that day. I would force myself to think only about that one thing and none of the other projects lying in wait. With a little help from friends and several dependable and affordable contractors, within half a year the lion's share of the work was complete, and with a couple of small windfalls, our financial situation reversed. Nearly two years into the loan we were able to refinance at a spectacularly low rate, saving us nearly ninety thousand dollars.

This is a long-winded way of saying that after I paused from being emotionally invested and reactive to my situation—and this is key—I recognized and admitted that fear had consumed me. It wasn't until I sought the help of God and friends that I became more capable of developing a game plan to overcome the obstacles I faced.

I: Identify Your Fear

Although it is a good first step to admit that you are afraid, it isn't enough to solve your problem and achieve your goals. It would not have been sufficient for me to acknowledge that I was afraid of failing to complete the remodel. It was also necessary to identify explicitly what I was afraid of. This process of getting to the bottom of my fear(s) was like unpeeling an onion. I identified several reasons for my fearful feelings. First was the fear of foreclosure. Digging a bit deeper, I realized that I was afraid of what my friends and family would think of me if I failed. I would look like the fool that Jesus mentioned in one of His parables, who set out to build the tower but could not complete the project because he didn't have the resources (see Lk 14:28-30).

After identifying concretely why I was afraid, it was far easier to address my fears logically by presenting those fears to people who could help me: my wife, my banker, and my spiritual director. But identifying your fears and naming them isn't always easy. Considering

Conquering F.E.A.R. with R.I.S.K.

this, I have developed a way to help, and it's G.O.L.D. I know, just what we need, another acronym.

Identify your fears by:

G: Ask yourself: what is my *Goal*? By understanding your goal, a lot of the minor setbacks move into the background. This helps you clarify what you actually want to achieve. Initially, I believed that my goal was to remodel the entire house. But after discussing the situation with my friend Kevin, Mr. Put on the Big-Boy Pants, I realized that far less needed to be completed than I thought, and that a lot of it could be completed by myself. And if I could not do it myself, I had time to save cash and hire a contractor who was right for the job.

O: What are the *Obstacles* that appear to be standing in the way of you achieving your goal(s)? By knowing your goal and seeing the obstacles that stand in the way of your goal, you can begin to systematically remove or overcome each obstacle one at a time. I had been trying to complete a multitude of projects at once. The scattered focus kept my wheels spinning but I was going nowhere. After I began to attack each project head-on from beginning to the end, or at least as far as I could go, things were completed with efficiency and excellence.

L: Ask yourself: what am I afraid of *Losing*? Remember that nearly every fear is born out of the potential of losing something we "love." In my case, my fears revealed that I loved my house and my pride in a disordered way that bordered on idolatry. When fear sets in, it can be very enlightening to think about what you're afraid of losing. Your answer may surprise you and reveal things about yourself that you knew but never wanted to admit. When you've answered this question, you can determine where what you "love" falls in the hierarchy of loves: first, God; second, your soul and your neighbor's soul; third, your body; and fourth, your possessions. Notice that my house falls under the least meaningful fourth category. Yet, my disproportionate fear of losing the house indicates that I was loving it more than my soul, and perhaps more than God . . . ouch.

D: Ask yourself: Why do you *Doubt?* This question can either be very easy to answer or nearly impossible to answer. Nevertheless it is important to make every effort to answer this question. *Where your doubt is, there also is your fear.* Kill the doubt and you kill your fear. You may doubt that your spouse loves you, that you are not needed by your friends and coworkers, that you may be terminated from your job, all the way to doubting that God cares for you.

If we apply the G.O.L.D. method to St. Peter walking on the water toward Christ, we can see how clarifying this process can be.

What was Peter's **Goal**: Was not to walk on water or to walk toward Christ (he accomplished both), but to actually get to Christ by walking on the water.

What were Peter's **Obstacles**: Waves and wind, gravity, his weight, perhaps his pride, and his lack of faith.

What was Peter afraid of **Losing?** His life, and perhaps his pride and honor.

What did Peter **Doubt?** God's power at work in him. He doubted that he could do what Jesus called him to do.

Almost always we will discover that the real obstacle to achieving our goal is not an extrinsic force, but an intrinsic reason: our doubt of ourselves and our abilities, or our doubt in God and His power in us.

S: Surrender Your Fear to God

This third step to overcoming your fears may seem to be a given. Many people say that they have surrendered their fears to God, only to continue to take them back for themselves. As the proverb says, the dog returns to its vomit (see Prv 26:11).

In this third step in the R.I.S.K. strategy we pause and pray to God. Our prayer consists of confessing our belief that God is sovereign. He can do anything in us, with us, and through us—but *He chooses* not to accomplish what He desires to achieve in us without us. In addition to believing in His sovereignty, we need to confess what we are afraid of losing *to Him*. This is important. By voicing our fear of losing something, we begin to see that thing we "love" as it is measured against God and His will for our lives. For example, I confess to God that I am afraid of losing my house. God then shows me that my inordinate fear of losing my house demonstrates that I "love" something that can't love me back, which is completely unreasonable. In fact, it may be sinful. By surrendering the potential loss of the house to God, I came to the conclusion that my body, my soul, my love for my wife and my family and God were still intact, and even if I did lose my house and had these things, I had nothing to fear.

By surrendering our fears to God, we begin to trust that He knows what is best for our lives. He may allow us to lose something that we love dearly. However, He permits this because He knows that it is better to lose an idol than to lose your soul. Regardless, God is generous, and though He may allow us to suffer loss, He will ensure that we have everything we need.

K: Kindle Trust in God by Taking Small Risks

Our Lord promises that those who are faithful in small matters will be granted greater responsibilities (see Lk 16:10). He also tells us to seek the Kingdom of God first

Conquering F.E.A.R. with R.I.S.K.

and all things will be granted to us besides (see Mt 6:33). If you are really praying and surrendering your fears to God and seeking His guidance, He will most surely give you a course of action.

But don't be fooled. God will not solve your problems immediately, or without your participation. He wants you to grow in trust in Him and increase in faith. To accomplish this, He gives us very small directives, things that appear to be insignificant, and asks us to do them.

Why? Because He wants you to grow in humility and obedience. The more humble and obedient you are, the more He can trust you with greater responsibilities. And the more He can trust you with, the more damage you can do to the evil one and his kingdom. The one who R.I.S.K.s penetrates the gates of hell, bringing Christ's light to those who are imprisoned in sin.

Naaman, the Syrian commander of armies of the king of Damascus, was a leper. Elisha the prophet sent a message to him telling him to wash seven times in the Jordan River and he would be healed. Naaman became enraged, because he desired that the prophet would wave his hand over the leprosy and command a dramatic healing. Naaman initially refused to follow Elisha's command, believing that the task was too insignificant. But upon the urging of his servant girl, he obeyed the prophet and was healed.

Do you want to be healed of your fears? Do you want the *inter**fear**ence* to stop undermining your ability to thrive? Obedience, especially to the small promptings of the Holy Spirit, is essential to conquering F.E.A.R. Why? Because when we are obedient to God in small matters, we begin to witness His grace working in our lives. We begin to perceive His fatherly care and provision. These little acts of obedience coupled with God's blessing forge a bond of trust between us and God. Each act of humble obedience in small matters is like kindling wood that is used to start a fire.

Have you ever tried to light a fire with a big slice of wood from a trunk of a tree? Even if you douse it with gas it rarely remains aflame for long. By using many little twigs we kindle a fire that allows us to burn larger logs.

Overcoming fear is similar to starting a campfire. God asks us to gather the little twigs, our little acts of obedience to His promptings. When we begin to see how He can make a fire out of our little actions, our trust in Him is ignited. With our faith aflame, He will then grant us greater logs to burn, greater responsibilities. It is then that we will be willing to face the fear of tremendous devilish things like persecutions and even martyrdom for the sake of Christ and His Gospel and the salvation of souls.

Toward the beginning of the year 2000, my third daughter, Anna Marie, was hospitalized at a children's hospital a couple of hours away from our home. I explained to my employer that Anna Marie was on life support, fighting for her little life, and I needed to take time off work to be with her. I asked him not to pay me because I did not know how long Anna's hospitalization would take. He assured me that there was no way that he wouldn't pay me.

After approximately two months, Anna Marie was released. I returned to my job, only to discover that my employer sold the company and the new owner was not pleased with my absence. Within days he canned me.

Prior to this, many of my prayers centered around asking God if I should start my own graphic design business. Well, I got my answer. I followed the "subtle"

Conquering F.E.A.R. with R.I.S.K.

prompting and opened shop. The phone didn't ring the entire season of Lent. I was nearly through the money that remained from my former job's last paycheck. This was it. I needed a miracle. I called an advertising firm that was looking for a graphic designer, and they said they would hire me immediately if I would relocate. I asked for some time to consider the opportunity.

After I hung up the phone, I closed the door to my office, fell to my knees, and looking at the crucifix hanging on my office wall, I begged God to show me what I should do. I sensed that I was called to have my own business, but it seemed hopeless. Should I take the job and relocate my family? I pleaded with God to do something. But instead, the words came to me: "*You* do something."

"You're kidding right? I have made cold calls, scouted potential new business opportunities, and nothing is working. What more do you want me to do?"

Another question penetrated my mind: "What do you want to do?" I responded, "Lord, since I surrendered my life to you, I have wanted to do graphic design for Catholic publishers and help build your kingdom." I sensed God saying, "Go do it."

I arose from prayer wondering who I could contact and what I would say. Fear began taking hold of me. I didn't think I could take any more rejection. Regardless, there was a nagging sense that this was a prompting of the Holy Spirit and I had better obey.

At that time, St. Joseph Communications was the largest Catholic publisher in America. I looked them up online and found a contact for the marketing director. I emailed him asking if they needed any help with their graphic design.

Within minutes, Richard, the vice president, responded, saying that my email came at the perfect time because that day two of their graphic designers quit. I didn't move. I stared at his email. I was in awe.

For the following eight years I was St. Joe's go-to graphic designer. Other Catholic publishers and authors saw my work and overnight I was providing graphic design and eventually branding for most of the major Catholic publishers and many prominent Catholic authors. But my desire to serve God more fully continued to increase.

During this time I wrote my first book, *Joseph's Way*, and sent it to one of the authors for whom I'd done graphic design. After reading it, he called me and asked, "Do you give talks?" To which I responded, "Brian, I don't even write, let alone give talks." Regardless, he invited me to address the men at one of his conferences. The talk was recorded. I shared it with another client, a prominent Catholic evangelist. He asked if he could distribute it. It wasn't long after that, that Lighthouse Catholic Media asked to distribute the talk. It went viral.

Soon after, people began requesting that I give talks around the nation. During this time, I realized that there was a massive hunger in men to know how they as fathers and husbands could live the Gospel of Jesus Christ. Responding to that need I founded the Fathers of St. Joseph, an apostolate that works for the restoration, redemption, and revitalization of fatherhood by following the timeless wisdom and ageless example of St. Joseph.

I produced more books and more talks, and eventually another Catholic client of mine introduced me to Stewardship: A Mission of Faith. Within a year I decided to leave my graphic design business and partner with Stewardship to work full time in the ministry of reaching fathers.

All because I rose from prayer and obediently sent an email to a person I had never met. That email was the kindling wood. And so were the other "yeses" along the way. God planted a burning desire in my heart to serve Him. But it took years of yearning, praying, hoping against all hope, and the overcoming of severe obstacles (including being rejected by a diaconate formation director who represented the Church and Christ) to kindle it. The little acts of surrender to God were the kindling of trust in Him. Responding to the Holy Spirit's promptings, I took little risks, and these little risks led to the fulfillment of that godly desire.

What is God calling you to do? What promptings have you received? Respond to them, regardless of how insignificant they seem. Have a filial, holy fear of God. Do not fear the worlds' hatred, but only fear displeasing your Father in heaven. Remember, "the one who fears is not perfect in love" (Jn 4:18). Kindle your trust in Him by responding to His promptings and take the calculated, prudential risks that He is asking of you. This will confirm your trust in Him, and eventually convince you of His love for you.

God is faithful and can do far more in you than you hope for or imagine (see Eph 3:20). Put on the mind of Christ, think with the Logos, and vanquish the devil's darts and the fear they instill, and believe that "I can do all things in Christ" (see Phil 4:13). If you R.I.S.K, the devil's *inter**fear**ence* will not be able to rattle your cage as it did previously. You will gradually experience the "freedom for which Christ has set you free" (see Gal 5:1). If you commit yourself to R.I.S.K., I guarantee you that your life will never be the same.

Endnotes

1. Summa Theologiae: Fear (Secunda Secundae partis, Q.125)
2. https://www.psychologytoday.com/us/blog/smashing-the-brainblocks/201511/7-things-you-need-know-about-fear
3. Summa Theologiae: The Gift of Fear (Secunda Secundae partis, Q.19)
4. https://www.psychologytoday.com/us/blog/smashing-the-brainblocks/201511/7-things-you-need-know-about-fear
5. Summa Theologiae: The Gift of Fear (Secunda Secundae partis, Q.19)
6. ibid
7. ibid
8. https://www.catholic.com/magazine/print-edition/the-seven-gifts-of-the-holy-spirit: Fear of God is, in this context, "filial" or chaste fear whereby we revere God and avoid separating ourselves from him—as opposed to "servile" fear, whereby we fear punishment (I/II.67.4; II/II.19.9).
9. Summa Theologiae: Fear (Secunda Secundae partis, Q.125)
10. To die to escape poverty, or lust or anything disagreeable means to seek a false way out of the difficult situation. St. Thomas is referring to the physical escape of situation by means of committing suicide, or possible the spiritual escape by avoid the confrontation of evil with holding fast to the good.
11. http://www.abrahamlincolnonline.org/lincoln/education/failures.htm
12. https://www.beliefnet.com/faiths/christianity/6-people-who-risked-everything-for-faith.aspx
13. Testimony taken by Gianni Giardinelli
14. ibid

WHAT IF I DON'T HAVE A PLAN FOR MY LIFE?
WE CAN HELP.

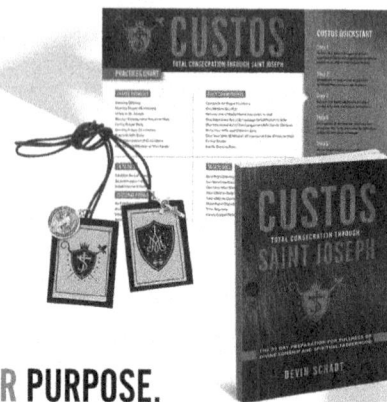

KNOW YOUR PURPOSE.
BUILD YOUR PLAN.
UNLOCK THE POWER.

The Fathers of St. Joseph has developed a plan that helps men know their noble purpose and unlock God's power in their lives. Access the tools to help you become who God intended you to be—like St. Joseph, a father on earth like the Father in Heaven at:

FATHERSOFSTJOSEPH.ORG